12 BIRDS
BACK FROM THE BRINK

by Nancy Furstinger

STORY
LIBRARY

www.12StoryLibrary.com

12-Story Library is an imprint of Peterson Publishing Company and Press Room Editions.

Produced for 12-Story Library by Red Line Editorial

Photographs ©: Daniel Brigginshaw/Shutterstock Images, cover, 1, 7; Ricardo Arduengo/AP Images, 4; Floridastock/Shutterstock Images, 6; Janelle Lugg/Shutterstock Images, 8, 9, 29; John Flesher/AP Images, 10; Minden Pictures/SuperStock, 11; Connie Barr/Shutterstock Images, 12; critterbiz/Shutterstock Images, 13; Steve Byland/Shutterstock Images, 14, 28; Gerald Marella/Shutterstock Images, 15; Keneva Photography/Shutterstock Images, 16; Cliff Collings/Shutterstock Images, 17; kohihirano/Shutterstock Images, 18; George Lamson/Shutterstock Images, 19; feathercollector/Shutterstock Images, 20; US Fish and Wildlife Service/AP Images, 21; New Zealand Conservation Department/AP Images, 22; Igor Golovniov/Shutterstock Images, 23; Jack Jeffrey/US Geological Survey, 24; Caleb Slemmons, 25; Chris Hill/Shutterstock Images, 26; Teri Verbickis/Shutterstock Images, 27

ISBN
978-1-63235-001-5 (hardcover)
978-1-63235-061-9 (paperback)
978-1-62143-042-1 (hosted ebook)

Library of Congress Control Number: 2014937274

Printed in the United States of America
Mankato, MN
June, 2014

Go beyond the book. Get free, up-to-date content on this topic at 12StoryLibrary.com.

TABLE OF CONTENTS

COLORFUL PUERTO RICAN PARROTS SOAR ONCE AGAIN

Puerto Rican parrots have flashy colors. Their green feathers are tipped with blue. These parrots gather in flocks and squawk loudly. They nest in holes in tall trees. They search for food in the forest's canopy. But their numbers started to fall after humans came on the scene.

Puerto Rican parrots settled the main island of Puerto Rico long before people arrived. Approximately 1 million parrots lived on the island at the beginning of the 1500s. But over time, they began to face many dangers. People trapped the parrots. They sold them as pets and as food. Red-tailed hawks ate their eggs and chicks. Hurricanes blew down some of the

parrots' nesting trees. New trees became hard to find after people cut down forests for farms. Farmers planted citrus trees, coffee plants, and sugar cane. By 1975, only 13 Puerto Rican parrots were left in the wild.

Several government agencies in Puerto Rico and the United States worked together to start the Puerto

Puerto Rican parrots are the only parrots native to the United States.

IUCN RED LIST

The International Union for the Conservation of Nature (IUCN) keeps a list of all threatened species in the world, called the Red List. Each species is labeled according to how at risk it is.

Least Concern: Not considered at risk.

Near Threatened: At risk of being vulnerable or endangered in the future.

Vulnerable: At risk of extinction.

Endangered: At high risk of extinction.

Critically Endangered: At extremely high risk of extinction.

Extinct in the Wild: Only lives in captivity.

Extinct: No members of a species are left.

Rican Parrot Recovery Program. This program was launched in 1972 to help the parrots recover in the wild so they would no longer be endangered. Scientists collected eggs and chicks from the wild. They raised the parrots in aviaries. The first chick was born in 1979. It took scientists years to learn more about the birds and how to hatch them. The more scientists learned, the more successful they became. By 2013, almost 400 parrots were being raised in captivity.

Later, the scientists released some parrots in the Rio Abajo State Forest and El Yunque National Forest in Puerto Rico. The parrots started building nests in the forests and hatching chicks. By 2013, more than 100 birds could be tracked in the wild. Another 400 lived in captivity.

7
Number of years it took for the first chick to be born in captivity.

Status: Critically endangered
Population: Approximately 100 in the wild
Home: Puerto Rico
Life Span: Up to 50 years

BALD EAGLES MAKE A BIG COMEBACK

Bald eagles have wings that span up to eight feet (2.4 m). These large birds use their strong talons to fish. They also use them to snare prey, such as raccoons. Bald eagle pairs mate for life. They build huge stick nests where they tend to their eggs. But pesticides threatened the eagles' ability to hatch eggs.

A new pesticide called DDT started being used in 1939. People used it to kill insects that spread diseases or destroyed crops. But DDT also washed into lakes and rivers and poisoned the fish. Bald eagles ate the fish. The chemicals in DDT caused the eagles' eggs to have very thin shells. The shells broke open before the chicks were ready to hatch.

Once, hundreds of thousands of bald eagles soared across the United States. They became America's national bird in 1782. But by 1963, their numbers had fallen to 417 nesting pairs. They were listed as endangered in 1973. The Environmental Protection Agency banned DDT in 1972. The Clean Water Act was also passed

Bald eagles can most often be spotted near bodies of water.

The bald eagle is one of the largest raptor species.

in 1972. It limited the amount of pollution going into waterways where eagles fished.

As their food sources became safer, bald eagles made a comeback. In 2007, they were taken off the US Endangered Species List. At that time, more than 10,000 breeding pairs were nesting across the United States.

7,000
Number of feathers a bald eagle has.

Status: Least concern
Population: Approximately 10,000 breeding pairs
Home: North America
Life Span: 15–30 years

KING PENGUIN NUMBERS ON THE RISE

King penguins get around by gliding through the water or sliding quickly on their bellies across the slick ice. Four layers of feathers keep them warm. During harsh winter storms, sometimes thousands of king penguins will huddle together for warmth. A mated pair will work hard to protect its egg from the cold.

The parents take turns balancing the egg on their feet. There the egg is warmed by their bellies. The chick hatches after 60 days.

King penguins live on islands north of the Antarctic. Hundreds of thousands of king penguins lived on Australia's Macquarie Island. People

Breeding colonies can range in size from dozens to thousands of king penguins.

discovered this island in 1810.
During the 1800s, hunters killed
3 million penguins for their blubber.
This was used for lamp oil. Hunting
was banned in 1919. By then,
approximately 4,000 king penguins
were left on the island.

In 1933, the island became a wildlife
sanctuary where king penguins and
other species were protected. Limits
were also put on fishing to protect
the penguins' food source. With
these protections, the population of
king penguins on Macquarie Island
has grown to approximately 100,000
mating pairs.

1,125
Depth in feet (343 m) that a king penguin can dive to get fish and squid to eat.

Status: Least concern
Population: More than
2 million mating pairs,
including 100,000
mating pairs on
Macquarie Island
Home: Macquarie Island
and other islands north
of the Antarctic
Life Span: 15–20 years

THINK ABOUT IT

King penguins are thriving
on many islands. Why do
you think it was important
to protect the species on
Macquarie Island?

FOREST FIRES HELP KIRTLAND'S WARBLERS GROW

Kirtland's warblers only make their nests in young jack pine trees in and around Michigan. The trees have to be between six and 22 years old. Scientists think the age of the tree matters because warblers need low tree branches to hide their nests. Before six years, the low branches are not big enough. Later, they start falling off. Once this happens, the warblers have to move to younger trees. But jack pine trees will only open their cones and spread their seeds after a fire. When humans started controlling forest fires, new trees stopped growing. The warblers were running out of places to nest.

Kirtland's warblers are songbirds. Their call sounds like "chip-chip-che-way-oh."

9

Age in days at which the chicks first leave the nest.

Status: Near threatened
Population: More than 2,000 males
Home: Michigan, Wisconsin, and Ontario, Canada
Life Span: 5–7 years

Kirtland's warblers eat flying insects, grasses, and berries.

People used to think that fires were bad for a habitat. Later, scientists realized naturally occurring fires serve a purpose, such as clearing space for new trees to grow. Without fires, the warblers lost their nesting trees. Their population fell from more than 1,000 in 1961 to approximately 400 in 1971. They were listed as endangered in 1967.

Conservationists wanted the birds to return. They started managing the forest in the 1970s using controlled burns. In a controlled burn, a team of experts starts a fire and then carefully keeps it under control. The heat of these fires lets the pinecones open so the seeds will spread.

As new trees grew, the warblers started to nest again. People are now able to count the male warblers by their singing voices. The females are not counted because they do not sing. The number of males rose to more than 2,000 in 2012. The warblers also have started to spread to Wisconsin and Canada to nest.

5

WHOOPING CRANES BOUNCE BACK FROM NEAR EXTINCTION

Whooping cranes are the tallest birds in North America. They stand almost five feet (1.5 m) tall. These birds have long legs and necks. This helps them to forage for plants, fish, and frogs in shallow water. The cranes live in family groups. Baby cranes can walk and swim soon after they hatch. Whooping cranes nearly became extinct when people hunted them and drained their wetlands.

Whooping cranes nest in Canada and spend winters on the Gulf Coast of Texas. They have always been rare. Scientists think their population may never have been more than 20,000. The number fell dangerously low when people started hunting them in the 1800s. The whooping cranes also lost habitat when people filled in the marshes to grow crops. The number fell to approximately

When flying, a whooping crane stretches its long neck out in front of its body.

Whooping cranes are named for the loud "whooping" sounds they make.

MATING DANCE

Whooping cranes dance to attract mates. Both cranes dance side by side. They run and leap. They flap their giant wings and toss their heads. They even fling feathers and sticks. They sing a duet of loud calls. Each pair will stay together for life.

1,400 by 1860. In 1941, only 15 whooping cranes could be found.

Many groups are working hard to bring up the number of cranes. A wildlife research center in Maryland was the first to start breeding them in captivity in 1967. The young cranes are released in Wisconsin and given a new winter home in Florida. In 2001, the nonprofit organization Operation Migration started teaching the released birds to migrate. Pilots fly in ultra-light aircraft to lead the way. More than 500 whooping cranes flew from Wisconsin to their winter habitat in Florida in 2009.

90
Whooping crane's wingspan in inches (2.3 m).

Status: Endangered
Population:
  Approximately 500
Home: North America
Life Span: 22–24 years

13

NEST BOXES BRING BACK EASTERN BLUEBIRDS

Eastern bluebirds live east of the Rockies, from Canada to Mexico. They fly south in the winter and are one of the first birds to return north in the spring. After returning, the female half of a mating pair takes approximately 10 days to build a cup-shaped nest. When it's done, she lays one light blue egg each day until she has approximately four or five in the nest. After approximately two weeks, they hatch. Both parents feed the young birds insects until they are old enough to leave the nest. But other birds have forced bluebirds from their homes.

Bluebirds like to build their nests in old woodpecker holes. Birds such as house wrens battle them for control of these holes. House wrens are

The eastern bluebird is the state bird of Missouri and New York.

Eastern bluebirds perch on posts or branches in open spaces to scan for prey.

tiny but strong. They drag bluebird eggs and young out of nests. Then they take over. The bluebirds that once were a common sight almost disappeared by the mid-1950s.

In 1979, an article in *Parade* magazine pointed out ways to save the bluebird. It asked readers to send in a quarter to receive plans for building special nesting boxes. More than 80,000 readers responded. Many people built the nesting boxes. They were placed on fence posts in open spots. House wrens nest in wooded areas, so they did not bother to nest in the boxes. The

eastern bluebirds thrived in their new homes. In 2012, the population was estimated at 22 million.

2
Notes that an eastern bluebird sings. It sounds like "too-lee."

Status: Least concern
Population: Approximately 22 million
Home: Eastern North America
Life Span: 6–10 years

BROWN PELICANS MAKE FULL RECOVERY

When they are fishing, brown pelicans plunge into the water. Then they scoop up fish into their throat pouch. This pouch hangs below the pelican's long beak and acts like a net. When it is full of water and fish, the pelican rises to the surface. It tips back the pouch to drain out the water, leaving behind the fish. In the 1950s, some of these fish turned out to be poisoned.

A brown pelican's beak can hold approximately three times as much as its stomach can.

3

Gallons (11 L) of water that the brown pelican's throat pouch can hold.

Status: Least concern
Population:
    Approximately 24,000
Home: North and South America
Life Span: 10–25 years

Brown pelicans have one of the longest bills of any bird. It measures 15–20 inches (38–51 cm).

Brown pelicans are the state bird of Louisiana. Thousands of the birds started dying in that state in the 1950s. Scientists found out a pesticide called Endrin had washed into rivers and the ocean. The fish in these waters were poisoned. Then pelicans ate the fish. The pesticide built up in the pelicans' bodies until they died.

The US government banned Endrin in 1986. Many pelicans had survived on Pelican Island off the Florida coast, where the pesticide had not reached. Some of these were sent to Louisiana between 1968 and 1980. They were last counted from helicopters in 2007. The count showed approximately 24,000—more than the state had in 1930, before Endrin was used.

SKY DIVERS

Brown pelicans can dive into the water from 65 feet (20 m) above. To protect themselves from the impact when they hit the water, they fill sacs under their skin with air. These cushions of air protect the pelicans' organs from harm.

CALIFORNIA CONDORS BACK TO SCAVENGING

California condors have no feathers on their heads. That is because these birds are scavengers. They eat dead animals, and bald heads help them to stay clean. They eat meat from the carcasses of large animals, such as deer or sheep. Sometimes, they will feed on smaller birds or rodents. But when humans developed the land the birds flew over, meals became harder to find.

California condors are the largest flying birds in North America. Their wings span up to 10 feet (3 m). These big birds need lots of space. They might travel 150 miles (241 km) every day to find a meal. Much of the open land that they soared over in California was developed into cities or farmland. Some condors also got lead

California condors can sometimes be spotted at Grand Canyon National Park.

poisoning when they fed on deer that had been killed by lead shotgun pellets.

In 1987, conservationists caught the last 22 condors in the wild. They bred them at zoos. In 1992, some of these birds began to be released in the wild. In 2011, a condor sanctuary on the coast of California provided the condors with 80 acres (32 ha) of space. Some deer hunters have switched to non-lead bullets to protect the condors' food supply. In 2013, the number of condors in the wild had risen to 435 worldwide. Of these, 237 condors were flying over California, Arizona, and Baja California, Mexico.

A young condor stays in its parents' nest until it is five or six months old.

15,000
Height in feet (4,572 m) that California condors can fly above land.

Status: Critically endangered
Population: 435 in the wild
Home: United States and Mexico
Life Span: Up to 60 years

PUPPET FEEDING

Zoo workers raised baby condors in breeding programs. The workers fed the baby birds with puppets that looked like bald condor heads. They did this so that the condors would bond with other condors, not people, before being released into the wild.

RED-COCKADED WOODPECKERS RETURN

Red-cockaded woodpeckers make their nests in live pine trees. They spend up to three years making nest holes. The birds flick layers of bark off the trees. Then they use their sharp beaks like chisels to chip a hole into the wood. Sticky sap drips out as the birds dig. This sap keeps snakes that climb trees away from the nests. Then loggers cut many of the pine trees down.

THINK ABOUT IT

Other species of birds like to use old woodpecker holes for nesting. How do you think these other birds were affected when the woodpeckers lost their habitat?

Red-cockaded woodpeckers make their nesting holes in aging pine trees because the decaying wood is softer.

The woodpeckers had fewer places to nest.

Loggers had been cutting down pine forests in the Southeast United States since approximately 1870. In 1970, the red-cockaded woodpeckers were listed as endangered. Conservation groups worked together to restore the woodpeckers' habitat. They planted new pine trees. Some of these trees were on private land or at military bases, while others were in national forests.

The new pine trees would take many years to grow. And it would take more years for the woodpeckers to dig out nest holes. So US wildlife officials gave the birds a head start. They made nest boxes and hammered these boxes into the trunks of small pine trees. Woodpeckers could start laying eggs in the nest boxes. In the first 10 years of the program, the population grew by 30 percent, to approximately 6,000. Since then, their numbers have risen to approximately 15,000.

26
Number of days that chicks remain in the nest hole.

Status: Near threatened
Population:
   Approximately 15,000
Home: Southeast United
   States
Life Span: Up to 12 years

Males have a red patch behind their eyes that gives these woodpeckers their name.

KAKAPO PARROTS WADDLE BACK FROM EXTINCTION

Kakapo parrots are the only nocturnal parrots, meaning they are active at night. They are also the only parrot that doesn't fly. Kakapo parrots mostly live on two islands in New Zealand, where they did not have any natural predators. That changed when people arrived on the islands and brought other animals with them.

The first people to arrive thousands of years ago chopped down trees where the parrots lived. They hunted the parrots for food. They made cloaks out of the feathers. In the 1800s, European settlers arrived, bringing cats and rats with them. Because the Kakapo parrots nest on the ground and do not fly, the new animals caught them easily. In the

Kakapo parrots are sometimes called owl parrots or night parrots.

ON DISPLAY

Europeans sent a Kakapo skin back to England in the late 1800s to be studied. Many museums wanted this strange parrot on display. Hunters started killing more of the birds to sell to museums and private collectors. So many parrots had been shipped to England by the early 1930s that collectors no longer wanted them. The birds ended up being used in dog food.

early 1900s, the birds were thought to be extinct.

In the 1970s, small populations of Kakapo parrots were found on far-off islands. But rats and cats were starting to prey on the birds there, too. Conservationists trapped the birds and moved them to

islands without predators. They gave the birds extra food to help them lay eggs more often. The population has risen to approximately 127.

5

Number of islands where Kakapo parrots have been relocated since 1975.

Status: Critically endangered
Population: Approximately 127
Home: New Zealand
Life Span: More than 60 years

The Kakapo appeared on a New Zealand stamp to raise awareness of the species.

0c

NEW ZEALAND

PALILAS NEST ON HAWAIIAN VOLCANO

Palilas, a kind of finch, can only be found on one volcano on Hawaii's Big Island. They live on the upper slopes of Mauna Kea, which has not erupted in 4,600 years. The palilas whistle a short song while they look for seeds of the Mamane tree and moth larvae. At dawn and dusk, their calls are louder and sharper. But new species brought to the island almost silenced the palilas' songs.

In the late 1700s, European farmers brought livestock to Hawaii.

Sheep and goats grazed on flowering plants that the birds depended on. Cats and rats ate palila eggs. Grasses planted by settlers stopped the Mamane tree, the palilas' main food source, from growing.

Palilas were listed as endangered in 1966. But little was done to save the birds until 1978. That's when an environmental group went to court to protect the birds. The court ruled that Hawaii had to prevent further damage to their habitat. The state

The palilas' song gets louder when rain is approaching.

A palila measures approximately six inches (15 cm) tall.

had to put up fences to keep livestock out of the palilas' habitat. The fences enclosed approximately 60,000 acres (24,000 ha) of land. Conservationists also caught some of the birds and released them on the other side of the volcano to try to expand their habitat. The first flock flew back. But many from the second flock stayed and started building nests.

12

Distance in miles (19 km) that the relocated flock flew home.

Status: Critically endangered
Population: 1,200
Home: Hawaii's Big Island
Life Span: Approximately 13 years

POISON SEEDS

Palilas live on the green seedpods of the Mamane tree. These seeds are very bitter. They are also poisonous. The seeds can kill a house finch within minutes. But palilas are able to eat the seeds without getting ill. One kind of caterpillar can also eat the seeds. The birds also eat these caterpillars.

PEREGRINE FALCONS BOUNCE BACK WITH BIGGER NUMBERS

Peregrine falcons fly faster than any other bird. They dive at speeds of more than 200 miles per hour (322 km/h). The falcons chase after smaller birds, such as pigeons. They catch the birds in mid-flight and kill them with a bite to the neck. But when their prey started to be poisoned, falcons' numbers took a nosedive.

In the mid-1900s, people used DDT on fields and marshes. This spray killed insects. When small birds ate the insects, the poison stayed in their bodies. Then falcons ate the small birds. The DDT built up in their bodies. It made the shells of their eggs very thin. The eggs cracked before they were ready to hatch. By the 1960s, few peregrine falcons were left in the United States.

The Peregrine Fund was started in 1970 to help the falcons. The fund helped

Peregrine falcons have a wingspan of more than three feet (0.9 m).

Peregrine falcons are known for their hooked beaks and sharp talons.

scientists to breed peregrine falcons in captivity to boost their numbers. The falcons lived in special chambers. They were fed vitamins to help the females lay strong eggs. The use of DDT was banned in 1972. After that, the young falcons could live in the wild again. Peregrine falcons were released around the United States. Their numbers climbed higher than they were before DDT came into use.

4,000
Number of falcons that the Peregrine Fund bred and released from 1974 to 1997.

Status: Least concern
Population: Approximately 3,000 nesting pairs in the United States
Home: All continents except Antarctica
Life Span: 17 years

THINK ABOUT IT

Birds of prey such as peregrine falcons are an important link in several food chains. They eat smaller birds, and other species eat the falcons' eggs. What do you think happens to the other species when this link is removed?

FACT SHEET

- While some bird species have made comebacks, many more are still in danger. The International Union for the Conservation of Nature lists 397 species of birds as endangered. Four others are extinct in the wild, and 198 are critically endangered.

- Many countries have laws protecting endangered animals. In 1973, the US Congress passed the Endangered Species Act. It requires state and federal government agencies to monitor and protect species that might become extinct. It also bans people from hunting, catching, trading, or possessing animals and plants that are protected.

- Pet cats kill an estimated 4 million birds every day in North America. Keeping pet cats indoors can limit this number.

- The two US federal agencies that deal with endangered species are the US Fish and Wildlife Service and the National Oceanic and Atmospheric Administration. Both have departments dedicated to identifying and helping endangered species.

- Several nonprofit organizations have been created to help threatened bird species. These nongovernmental groups include the American Bird Conservancy, the National Audubon Society, The Nature Conservancy, Partners in Flight, and the Royal Society for the Protection of Birds.

- Birds around the world have been affected by climate change. Warmer temperatures have caused habitat loss, especially near the North Pole and South Pole. Changing weather patterns have reduced birds' ability to reach their breeding grounds on time. Climate change could soon affect king penguins. When seas warm up, the penguins' food supply shrinks. Then these birds will have to travel greater distances to find the squid and lantern fish that they eat.

- Bald eagles are no longer considered an endangered species. But they remain protected under the Bald and Golden Eagle Protection Act and the Migratory Bird Treaty Act. These laws protect eagles, their nests, and their eggs.

- Bird lovers continue to help the bluebirds by keeping an eye on nest boxes. They visit the nests and record what they find. They take photos and videos of nesting birds. Some have even made roosting boxes where birds can keep warm in winter.

- The red-cockaded woodpeckers are the only woodpeckers to make homes in living trees. Other birds, such as screech owls, sometimes move into old nest holes. Raccoons, flying squirrels, bees, and wasps also claim the holes.

GLOSSARY

aviary
A protected place where birds are kept.

blubber
The fat of large sea mammals, such as whales.

breeding
The process by which animals or plants are produced by their parents.

canopy
Treetops in a forest that form a kind of ceiling.

conservationist
Someone who preserves, manages, and cares for the environment.

endangered
Threatened with extinction.

extinction
The death of all members of a species.

habitat
The place where a plant or animal naturally lives or grows.

migrate
To travel from one habitat to another.

pesticide
A chemical used to kill insect pests.

predator
An animal that kills or eats another animal.

prey
An animal that is killed or eaten by another animal.

sanctuary
A place where wildlife are protected from predators and people.

scavenger
An animal or bird that feeds on dead and rotting flesh.

threatened
At risk of becoming endangered.

FOR MORE INFORMATION

Books

Alderfer, Jonathan. *Bird Guide of North America*. Washington, DC: National Geographic Children's Books, 2013.

Boothroyd, Jennifer. *Endangered and Extinct Birds*. Minneapolis: Lerner, 2014.

George, Jean Craighead, and Wendell Minor. *The Eagles Are Back*. New York: Dial, 2013.

Haywood, Karen. *Hawks and Falcons*. Salt Lake City: Benchmark Books, 2010.

Roth, Susan L., and Cindy Trumbore. *Parrots over Puerto Rico*. New York: Lee & Low Books, 2013.

Websites

Discovery Kids: Birds
kids.discovery.com/tell-me/animals/birds

National Geographic Kids: Animals and Nature
kids.nationalgeographic.com/kids/stories/animalsnature

San Diego Zoo Kids: Birds
kids.sandiegozoo.org/animals/birds

US Fish & Wildlife Service: Endangered Species for Kids
www.fws.gov/endangered/education

INDEX

About the Author

Nancy Furstinger is the author of almost 100 books, including many on animals. She has been a feature writer for a daily newspaper, a managing editor of trade and consumer magazines, and an editor at two children's book publishing houses.

READ MORE FROM 12-STORY LIBRARY

Every 12-Story Library book is available in many formats, including Amazon Kindle and Apple iBooks. For more information, visit your device's store or 12StoryLibrary.com.